INVESTIGATE BIODIVERSITY

Kristen Rajczak Nelson

AMPHIBIANS

Enslow Publishing
101 W. 23rd Street
Suite 240
New York, NY 10011
USA
enslow.com

•• Words to Know

adaptation A change in an animal that happens over a long time. It helps the animal survive.

developed To be more grown.

ecosystem The living and nonliving things in an area.

ectothermic Cold-blooded; having a body temperature that changes with the environment.

habitat The place where an animal lives.

humid Having a lot of water in the air.

larva The early form of an animal. It usually does not look like the adult form.

mate To come together to make babies.

mucus A thick, wet matter that is made by the body.

predator An animal that hunts and eats other animals.

survive To continue to live.

vertebrate An animal with a backbone.

Contents

What Makes an Amphibian?

Amphibians are amazing animals! The word "amphibian" means "double life." That's because amphibians spend part of their life on land and part of their life in the water.

Fascinating Features

Animals in the amphibian group have some things in common. All amphibians are **vertebrates**, or have a backbone. Most of them have thin, soft skin that needs to be kept wet. They may have **mucus** on their skin to keep it moist. Amphibians don't have scales. They are able to take in water through their skin because it's so thin.

All amphibians are **ectothermic**. This means they are cold-blooded. Their body temperature changes depending on how warm or cold it is around them. Amphibians have to find

Frogs are one kind of amphibian. All amphibians live on land as well as in water.

Getting Air

Amphibians do have lungs. But their skin is so thin that gases can move through it. This means amphibians can breathe through their skin!

a sunny spot to warm up. They're more active when they're warm. To cool down, they head to shady spots or underground. Most amphibians hatch from eggs, too.

The eastern red-spotted newt is often found in forests.

The Chinese giant salamander is the largest amphibian in the world.

All Shapes and Sizes

There are thousands of different species, or kinds, of amphibians. They all share some main features. But they can look and act very different. Some are tiny. The Brazilian gold frog is less than 0.5 inch (1.3 centimeters) long. Amphibians can also be very large. The Chinese giant salamander can be up to 6 feet (1.8 meters) long! There are so many kinds of amphibians. It can be lots of fun to learn about this animal group!

Who Lives Where?

Most amphibians have a special kind of **habitat**. This is where they live. They like to be near water because they need to keep their skin wet. They may also live in places that are very **humid**. This means there is a lot of water in the air. Still, amphibians can be found in places all over the world. They are more likely to live in places that are warm. Amphibians may live on the forest floor or even in trees! They're found on mountains and in rain forests.

Frogs and Toads

There are three main groups of amphibians. Frogs and toads are the biggest group. Adult frogs and toads have four legs and are known for hopping! They have some differences, too. Frogs often live in water, while toads just live close to water. Frogs have slimy, smooth skin. Toads have dry and bumpy skin.

The common toad can be found in many parts of the world.

Salamanders

Salamanders are another group of amphibians. Salamander adults have four legs and a tail. Newts are part of this group, too. Newts spend a lot of time living on land. Mudpuppies and axolotls are two special kinds of salamanders.

Digging In

Amphibians in the desert have special ways of living with little water. The desert spadefoot toad has large feet shaped like a shovel. He uses them to dig a hole to hide from the sun for months at a time!

The Corsican fire salamander lives on the island of Corsica in the Mediterranean Sea.

The South American caecilian spends most of its time underground.

Caecilians

Caecilians are the smallest group of amphibians. They are the only amphibians that don't have legs. They look a lot like big earthworms! They have tiny eyes. They may even be under their skin. Sometimes it's hard to tell which end of a caecilian is its head. Caecilians mostly live underground or underwater. Scientists don't know a lot about them.

Amphibian Life

All amphibians have a life cycle. Some parts are alike. All amphibians need a male and female to **mate**. This is how they have babies. Many baby amphibians hatch from eggs laid by an adult female. Most amphibians have **larvae** that live in water. They do not look like adults of their kind. Larvae go through a change to become adults. It is called metamorphosis.

Hatching and Growing

Amphibians may have special **adaptations**. These help them **survive** in their habitat. Frogs may lay thousands of eggs at a time. Salamanders only lay about one hundred eggs.

A cluster of frog eggs

13

Some salamanders' eggs even hatch inside the mother's body! Frogs start out as larvae. They are called tadpoles. They look more like a fish. They may stay like this for weeks or months. It depends on the kind of frog. Salamander larvae start to grow legs and look like adults after about two months.

Great Gills

Amphibian larvae have gills. They help them breathe in the water. They often lose the gills as they grow into adults. Adult amphibians more often live on land. They do not need gills.

This blotched tiger salamander is in its larval stage.

Caecilian Babies

Some caecilians have a life cycle that is a lot like frogs and salamanders. They hatch from eggs. They live as larvae in water. Then they become adults. But many caecilians don't lay eggs at all! Instead, they are more like humans. They give birth to live babies. The babies are already well **developed** when they are born.

A salamander dines on a worm.

Meal Time

Amphibian young eat a lot! They need lots of food while they're growing from larvae to adults. What they eat depends on their species. Often their food is different from what adults eat. Tadpoles may eat plants, algae, and other tadpoles. Adult frogs eat bugs. Salamander larvae hunt for tiny water animals to eat. Adult salamanders eat worms and bugs of many kinds.

Adapting to Survive

Amphibians have lots of differences. This is because of their adaptations. Some adaptations have to do with the body. Amphibians can have all different shapes, sizes, or parts. Other adaptations have to do with how the animal acts. All adaptations happen to help the animal survive in its habitat.

Adapting to Survive

Adaptations may include the body parts used for eating. Frogs have a long, sticky tongue. This helps them grab bugs they like to eat. They also have teeth to hold on to their food!

Some adaptations help keep amphibians safe from **predators**. Caecilians have poisons in their skin. This can stop other animals from eating them. Sometimes an amphibian's skin lets predators know that it is poisonous. These amphibians have bright colors. Predators know they should stay away. In order to get away from a predator, some salamanders can drop their tails. Then, the tail can grow back!

A frog uses his long tongue to catch a nearby butterfly.

Staying Hidden

Camouflage helps an animal hide from predators. Camouflage can be colors or shapes that make the animal blend in with its habitat. This is another adaptation of many amphibians!

Amphibians in the Ecosystem

Frogs need bugs to eat. Salamanders need worms. In the same way, other animals need to eat amphibians. Fish eat amphibian larvae. Without predators to eat them, there would be too many amphibians. The **ecosystem** would be in trouble. But changes in a habitat can be extra hard on amphibians. Since their thin skin allows water and gases through, they can get sick from pollution or other changes. From garbage to a change in weather, these changes can cause amphibians to die out.

Amphibians have many amazing adaptations. The earth is always changing. This means amphibians will continue to change, too. Amphibians have tons of cool features, so there's always more to learn!

This salamander's bright colors warn predators to stay away.

Activity: Study Life Cycles!

●●● The life cycles of amphibians are so interesting because of how different they can be! Choose two amphibians you think are interesting. Do some research online about your amphibians. (Make sure you check with an adult first.) Write out the steps of their life cycles. Be sure to include how males and females find mates and the species' metamorphosis. Look at the life cycles side by side. Try to answer these questions:

- What is the same between the two amphibians?
- What are the differences?
- Can you think of **why** they might be similar or different?

The frog life cycle begins with two frogs mating. Then eggs hatch into tadpoles, which grow into adult frogs.

●●○ Learn More

Books

Bard, Mariel. *Amphibian Fossils*. New York, NY: PowerKids Press, 2017.

Jacobson, Bray. *Amphibian Life Cycles*. New York, NY: Gareth Stevens Publishing, 2018.

Ogden, Charlie. *Amphibians*. New York, NY: KidHaven Publishing, 2017.

Websites

Ducksters: Amphibians
www.ducksters.com/animals/amphibians.php
Learn more about amphibian features and life cycles and play some fun games.

National Geographic Kids: Amphibians
kids.nationalgeographic.com/animals/hubs/amphibians
Explore this website to learn about all kinds of amphibians.

●●○ Index

Published in 2019 by Enslow Publishing, LLC.
101 W. 23rd Street, Suite 240, New York, NY 10011

Library of Congress Cataloging-in-Publication Data
Names: Rajczak Nelson, Kristen, author.
Title: Amphibians / Kristen Rajczak Nelson.
Description: New York : Enslow Publishing, 2019. | Series: Investigate biodiversity | Audience: Grade K-4. | Includes bibliographical references and index.
Identifiers: LCCN 2018004934| ISBN 9781978501843 (library bound) | ISBN 9781978502383 (paperback) | ISBN 9781978502390 (6 pack)
Subjects: LCSH: Amphibians—Juvenile literature.
Classification: LCC QL644.2 .R34 2019 | DDC 597.8—dc23
LC record available at https://lccn.loc.gov/2018004934

Printed in the United States of America

Photos Credits: Cover, pp. 1, 5 Kurit afshen/Shutterstock.com; pp. 3, 19 Cathy Keifer/Shutterstock.com; pp. 3, 16 Kenneth M Highfill/Science Source/Getty Images; pp. 3, 21 Choke29/Shutterstock.com; pp. 3, 9 davemhuntphotography/Shutterstock.com; pp. 3, 11 Beatrice Prezzemoli/Shutterstock.com; p. 6 gary powell/Shutterstock.com; p. 7 tristan tan/Shutterstock.com; p. 12 Dante Fenolio/Science Source/Getty Images; p. 13 Marco Maggesi/Shutterstock.com; p. 15 Jay Fleming/Corbis Documentary/Getty Images; p. 23 GraphicsRF/Shutterstock.com; cover graphics magic pictures/Shutterstock.com.